MY WORLD OF
COLOR

Red, yellow, green, and blue
Blue is the door
That takes you through

Into . . .

Margaret Wise Brown
MY WORLD
COL

OF

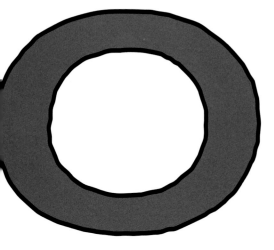

OR

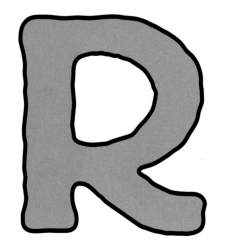

PICTURES BY

Loretta Krupinski

SCHOLASTIC INC.
New York Toronto London Auckland Sydney
Mexico City New Delhi Hong Kong Buenos Aires

Red as roses
Red as red
Red as the eyes
In a rabbit's head

Orange as an orange tree
Orange as a bumblebee
Orange as the setting sun
Sinking slowly in the sea

Yellow as a daisy's eye
Or a cabbage butterfly
Or the stripes across a bee
And every dandelion I see

Green as a grasshopper
Green as the green
Of the greenest fern
Any rabbit has seen

Blue as the ocean
Blue as the sky
Blue as a bluebird
Flying by

Purple as Easter eggs, marbles,
   and jellies
Purple as martins with purple bellies
Purple as coal and purple balloons
Purple as shadows of late afternoon

Brown as mahogany
Brown as a willow tree
Brown as old brooms
Brown as a ship's boom

Black as trees
Black as ink
Black as the night
Where the dark moles think

Gray as soft fur
Gray as gray socks
Gray as Grandmother
Gray as a fox

White as a dish
White as a fish
When you eat a
white fish
On a milk-white dish

Pink as pigs
Pink as toes
Pink as a rose

Or a rabbit's nose

Now, *I* can color

RED as roses

ORANGE as an orange tree

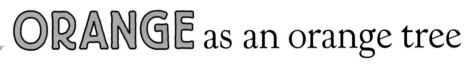

YELLOW as butter and bees

GREEN
as the grass

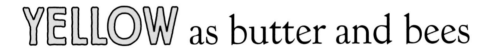

BLUE as the sky

PURPLE as phlox

GRAY as a fox

BLACK as a fly

PINK as a pig

BROWN as a tree

WHITE as the raging seas

Red, yellow, green, and blue
Blue is the door
That takes you through
Into . . .

Our world of
COLOR

ISBN 0-439-45065-9

12 11 10 9 8 7 6 5 4 3 2   2 3 4 5 6 7/0

Printed in the U.S.A   14

First Scholastic printing, September 2002

Designed by Christine Kettner